BROADWAY & HOLLYWOOD TOO

by Andrew A. Aros

applause publications   diamond bar

Published by APPLAUSE PUBLICATIONS
2234 South Shady Hills Drive
Diamond Bar, California 91765

L.C. 80-67670

ISBN: 0-932352-04-9

PRINTED IN THE UNITED STATES
OF AMERICA

For Joe,

who opened a new window

CONTENTS

INTRODUCTION

When Al Jolson delivered his famous "stick around folk, you ain't heard nothing yet" over that scratchy Vitagraph sound system, he was ushering in more than the era of talking motion pictures. For as the sound gradually improved, so did the accompanying images up there on the silver screen.

As we became more and more involved with our fantasies in the cavernous darkness of the movie palaces, music, it was found, could increase our responses tenfold. Prior to the onset of sound, few films had original music written for them. While most theaters featured musical accompaniment for their attractions, it was generally of an unimaginative nature--"Hearts and flowers", "Over the waves", "William Tell Overture", etc.

The theater organist, piano player, or transient musician, had to be versatile, since one moment sadness was the desired response, suspense the next, and a bit of comic relief following that. In the silent era, there were a few original scores written for the movies, but it was not until the arrival of sound that any serious thought was given to movie music.

While nearly every major studio offered some form of "all talking, all dancing, all singing" feature film in the beginning, Paramount and Warner Bros. seemed to understand the new medium better than most of the other studios. Warner Bros. was a particular trend setter, and their series of Busby Berkeley synchronized depression era musicals are still entertaining audiences a half century later.

Say Warner Brothers when discussing musicals, and such all-time favorites as 42nd Street, Footlight Parade, Flirtation Walk, or The Gold Diggers of 1933, readily come to mind. Yet, in the evolution of dramatic scores, Warner's was also instrumental introducing us to the work of such famous screen composers as Max Steiner, Alfred Newman, and Erich Wolfgang Korngold.

Broadway had existed long before Hollywood. From the days of Tin Pan Alley, the Ziegfeld Follies, George White Scandals, and other musical entertainments, our nation's musical tastes have often been shaped by what has appeared on that narrow strip of Manhattan real estate. Sharing a symbiotic relationship for musical properties, Hollywood and Broadway often seem worlds apart.

While Broadway performers often eschew and express disdain for the razzle dazzle glamour of Hollywood, there are few Broadway stars who have not tried their hand at acting in films. Many, in fact, have served an apprenticeship in Hollywood before going on to even greater fame on the Broadway boards, (i.e., Angela Lansbury, Lauren Bacall, Alexis Smith).

In this book we will examine many Broadway shows and their Hollywood adaptations. Additionally, we will also look at original motion picture scores, hopefully pointing out noteworthy examples of the best Hollywood has given us.

Since musical tastes are highly subjective, the choices of what have been included and excluded, are mine. My selections constitute what I feel are the best representative recordings of original cast and soundtrack albums.

I have chosen to include music which is presently available. I have not recommended anthologies (such as the excellent <u>Broadway Magic</u> series on Columbia), nor have I suggested rare, historic, or out-of-print performances.

This is a checklist of sorts, for the individual or institution, desiring a basic list against which their own holdings can be measured. Hopefully, this will be a handy shopping tool-selection guide that will enable you to fill in the gaps in your collection.

Whether one purchases one's recordings at a record shop or through Saturday morning garage sales and flea markets, the albums in this book speak for themselves with universal popularity, critical acclaim, and unique characteristics of quality, creativity, or seminal importance.

Find a comfortable seat and enjoy this book....the curtain's just going up!

BROADWAY

AIN'T MISBEHAVIN'.   2-RCA CBL2-2965.
    2 discs.

The music of Fats Waller forms the basis
of this musical. Those who enjoy the sounds
of ragtime (and who doesn't?) will find this
raucous score to their tastes. Only a hand-
ful of Black composers have made an impact
on the Broadway stage, and while Waller was
not noted for Broadway musicals, his contributions to American popular music cannot be
overlooked. This original cast recording
corrects that wrong by bringing Waller or-
iginals to our attention.

ANNIE. Columbia JS-34712. 1 disc.

Little Orphan Annie, who by now should
qualify for Medicare, was brought to life
on Broadway in the person of Andrea McArdle.
All the familiar characters of the comic
strip are here, from Annie's talented mutt
Sandy, to the loveable Daddy Warbucks. Even
FDR makes an appearance, joining the cast
in a chorus of "Tomorrow".

APPLAUSE. MCA OC-11. 1 disc.

Lauren Bacall made an electrifying
comeback in this musical version based
on the film classic, All About Eve.
Examining the conflict between two
women both on and off stage, Bacall's
bravura performance may well never
be equalled.

BARNUM. Columbia JS-36576. 1 disc.

The American musical theater has been
comatose for the past few years, and only
occasionally has it revived sufficiently
to let us know it's not dead yet. Barnum,
a bright ray of hope, contains a brilliant
score by Cy Coleman and lyrics by Michael
Stewart. It is one of those razzle dazzle
hits that one finds difficult to dislike.
Jim Dale plays the title role of the show
biz impressario, and he is the show.

BELLS ARE RINGING. Columbia Special Products
    AS-32608. 1 disc.

For the most part, the musical comedies
of the fifties were generally lackluster.
There were exceptions, though, and this
is one of them. Judy Holliday, Sydney
Chaplin, and Jean Stapleton were the stars,
while the team of Jule Styne, Betty Comden
and Adolph Green, wrote this success. An
adventure about a switchboard operator who
involves herself in the problems of her
clients, it was later made into a disappoint-
ing film.

BYE BYE BIRDIE. Columbia Special Products
COS-2025. 1 disc.

Chita Rivera and Dick Van Dyke were the
stars of this musical comedy by the reliable
Charles Strouse (music) and Lee Adams (lyrics)
team. With a book by Michael Stewart, the
ever-present familial tensions were parodied.
A rock and roll star, reminiscent of Elvis
Presley is drafted. This serves as the
catalyst for several enjoyable songs, "One
boy", "Spanish Rose", "Kids", "Put on a happy
face", and "What did I ever see in him".

CABARET. Columbia KOS-3040. 1 disc.

Sally Bowles has had many incarnations
--first as a character in a series of Christopher Isherwood short stories, and then in
John Van Druten's stage play, I am a camera,
which was later made into a movie. In 1966,
Sally again appeared, this time as the heroine
of a musical by the team of John Kander (music)
and Fred Ebb (lyrics), with a book by Joe
Masteroff. Dealing with life in Berlin on
the eve of the Nazi's rise to power, it was
far from the typical pastiche of songs, sequins,
and feathers that characterize most Broadway
productions. It touched on the inhumane
aspects of the Nazi's treatment of the Jews,
in an atmosphere that was fast becoming
decadent. With Jill Haworth in the principal
role, the show was all but stolen by the
appearances of Lotte Lenya and Joel Grey.
Several memorable numbers emerged, including
"Married", "Willkommen", etc. Joel Grey was
a somewhat sinister Master of Ceremonies,
and only he repeated his role in the film
version six years later.

CAMELOT.   Columbia JS-32602. 1 disc.

   Theatrical magic occurs rarely, and
when it does, it does not go unnoticed.
Richard Burton, Julie Andrews, and Robert
Goulet were at the core of this Alan Jay
Lerner (lyrics and book) and Frederick
Loewe (music) collaboration. Set in the
days of King Arthur and the Knights of
the Round Table, it became a favorite
of the newly inaugurated American president, John F. Kennedy. It boasted an
entire score that proved popular with
the general public as well--"The merry
month of May", "C'est moi", "If ever I
would leave you", "What do the simple
folks do?", and "Guinevere".

CHICAGO: A MUSICAL VAUDEVILLE.   Arista
   9005. 1 disc.

   Gwen Verdon and Chita Rivera were
joined by Jerry Orbach to form a creative
entertainment troika. No strangers to
Broadway, they had each established
reputations for themselves via a string
of hits. Set in the roaring twenties
in Chicago, we follow the fortunes of
two chorus girls. With a score by the
now familiar team of John Kander (music)
and Fred Ebb (lyrics), it would be
difficult to find reasons for not including this work in a collection of
Broadway's best.

A CHORUS LINE.   Columbia JS-33581. 1 disc.

   Whatever becomes of the thousands of
actors that audition in the cattle call
tryouts is the subject of this popular
musical. A Chorus Line attempts to show
the result, by presenting more than a
dozen vignettes told in song and dance.
The score is right on target, touching
and reaching theater audiences everywhere.

COMPANY.   Columbia OS-35550. 1 disc.

Stephen Sondheim has a way with lyrics, to say nothing of catchy melodies. The musical, with a book by George Furth, explores the often strange world of marital relationshionships, as seen through the eyes of an unmarried and very much in demand successful young man. Though witty and amusing in parts, it presented an often disturbing glimpse of the loneliness of contemporary urban life. Elaine Stritch was a standout with her serio-comic, "The ladies who lunch".

A DAY IN HOLLYWOOD, A NIGHT IN THE UKRAINE.
DRG SBL-12580. 1 disc.

Just about every film cliche one has ever heard, forms the basis for this pleasant comedy and entertainment. The first half is a salute to the film musicals of the depression era, with a medley of many familiar musical standards. A personal favorite is "Doin' the Production Code", in which the cast tap dance, while reciting portions of the ridiculous motion picture production code. The second half is a highly unlikely Marx Brothers scenario, rich with humor. Priscilla Lopez, David Garrison and Frank Lazarus head the highly talented cast.

EUBIE!   Warner Bros. HS-3267. 1 disc.

Eubie, like Ain't Misbehavin' is a tribute more than a straight musical. A pure joy, it celebrates many of the songs of one of America's overlooked Black songwriters, Eubie Blake, now in his nineties, and still very active. While most of us are familiar with "I'm just wild about Harry", this collection also includes lesser known hits.

EVITA.   MCA2-11007.   2 discs.

Eva Peron is one of the twentieth century's most colorful and controversial women. This Andrew Lloyd-Webber and Tim Rice musical captures her compelling and at times despotic personality, and like a modern day opera chronicles her rise from a life of poverty, to one of power, as the wife of Argentine dictator, Juan Peron. Adding the presence of Che Guevara gives the musical an almost surreal atmosphere. The score is strong, featuring "Don't cry for me Argentina", "Eva beware of the city", and "I'd be surprisingly good for you".   Patti LuPone, who plays Eva, is a standout.

THE FANTASTICKS.   MGM 3872.   1 disc.

Still playing off-Broadway where it has remained for more than a quarter of a century, this Harvey Schmidt (music) and Tom Jones (lyric and book) masterpiece is deceptively simple. Yet, it has enjoyed productions around the world, and audiences have thrilled to the score and its observations on human nature. Famed for introducing the song, "Try to remember", it is one of those shows that you will play time and time again.

FIDDLER ON THE ROOF.   RCA LSO-1093.   1 disc.

One would think that a musical dealing with the persecution of Jews in turn-of-the century czarist Russia would hardly be a suitable topic for a musical comedy, but Sheldon Harnick (lyrics) and Jerry Bock (music) somehow make it work, due in no small measure to Joseph Stein's well-paced book. The late Zero Mostel is the real star, and his Tevye is one of those rare jewels of characterization. Essential.

FOLLIES. Capitol SO-761. 1 disc.

This Stephen Sondheim musical about
the reunion of several showgirls in a
theater that is about to be torn down,
was the turning point in the career of
Alexis Smith, marking her return to the
stage after a stay in Hollywood that
lasted more than a decade.

FUNNY GIRL. Capitol STAO-2059. 1 disc.

Barbra Streisand was first seen by
Broadway audiences in I can get it
for you wholesale, and was selected to
play the part of Fanny Brice in this
Jule Styne (music) and Bob Merrill (lyrics)
musical that followed a determined young
singer/comedienne's rise from obscurity
to a leading role in the Ziegfeld Follies.
Sydney Chaplin plays gambler Nick Arnstein,
for whom Fanny falls and later weds. "Who
taught her everything", "I want to be seen
with you tonight", "Find yourself a man",
and "Rat-tat-tat-tat" are only a few of
the numbers in the stage version that did
not make it onto movie screens when it was
filmed four years later.

GEORGE M! Columbia KOS-3200. 1 disc.

Shortly after leaving Cabaret, in which
he nightly brought the house down, Joel
Grey was offered the lead in George M,
which purported to tell the story of Broadway's master showman, George M. Cohan.
Using original Cohan songs and music, it
soon became obvious to anyone that this
was more a revue than a musical comedy.
Joel Grey is the star, but he must also
share the chief billing honors with the
songs themselves, "Forty five minutes from
Broadway", "Over there", "Yankee Doodle
Dandy", etc.

GYPSY.   Columbia S-32607. 1 disc.

Jule Styne (music) and Stephen Sondheim
(lyrics) have given us one of Broadway's
most treasured musicals, and a role that
the great Ethel Merman could really sink
her teeth into (to not even mention her
voice!). The story of stripper, Gypsy
Rose Lee, her rocky relationship with her
mother, and her rise to stardom following
the death of vaudeville, furnished the
situations for some great songs--"Let me
entertain you", "All I need is the girl",
"You gotta have a gimmick", "Some people",
"Small world", etc. Ethel Merman, who
plays Gypsy's gutsy stage mother belts out
"Rose's turn" and "Everything's coming up
roses". Essential for all collections.

HAIR. RCA LSO-1150. 1 disc.

At the height of the Vietnam war, the
rock musical evolved, and Hair was the
best of them all! With music by Galt
MacDermot and lyrics and book by the
show's stars, Jerome Ragni and James Rado,
this was one of the hottest tickets on
Broadway. It touched on the generation
gap, drugs, race, sex, and of course, the
war. Songs such as "Aquarius", "Sodomy",
"I got life", "Easy to be hard", "Good
morning starshine", and the "Flesh failures
(let the sunshine in)", were but a few of
the highlights of this show, some of which
on to become top 40 hits for others. In
looking at but a few of the cast members
on the original recording, you will see
such names as Steve Curry, Paul Jabara,
Melba Moore, and Diane Keaton. The film
version of Hair was made a decade later,
and one could only speculate on what
impact it would have had on the war,
had the film been released in 1970.

HELLO, DOLLY!   RCA LSOD-2087. 1 disc.

For some, Carol Channing is the only
actress who can play Dolly Levi. But
audiences have seen such diverse per-
sonalities as Pearl Bailey (RCA ANL2-
2849), Mary Martin (RCA LSOD-2007),
Ginger Rogers, Martha Raye, and others
in the role. Carol Channing is enchant-
ing as ever, and makes the most of the
Jerry Herman score which includes "I put
my hand in", "Before the parade passes by",
and "So long dearie". Of course, her
showstopping "Hello, Dolly!" number never
fails to thrill, and even on disc, one
feels part of the Harmonia Gardens audience.
President Lyndon Johnson adapted the song
to "Hello, Lyndon" and used it in his
1964 election bid. Essential.

JESUS CHRIST SUPERSTAR.   MCA 5000. 1 disc.

With the exception of Hair, few musicals
with a rock score have enjoyed widespread
popularity or acceptance on Broadway.
Godspell, which appeared in the same season
as Jesus Christ Superstar was less dependent
on spectacle and didn't really exploit the
theatrical medium as did the latter. The
score for Superstar was equally dynamic,
featuring "I don't know how to love him"
and others. Written by Andrew Lloyd-Webber
(music) and Tim Rice (lyrics), a British
duo, whose later effort, Joseph and the
Technicolor dreamcoat failed to duplicate
their previous success, it was not until
Evita, that they were able to demonstrate
that JCS had not been a fluke.

THE KING AND I.   RCA ABL1-2610. 1 disc.

In 1977 when Rodgers and Hammerstein's classic musical was revived, it's original star Yul Brynner was lured and snagged to head the top of the bill. So closely had he come to be identified with his role as the King of Siam, that the public demanded that only he play the role. The score includes "Shall we dance", "Getting to know you", "Something wonderful", and "The March of the Siamese children".

A LITTLE NIGHT MUSIC. Columbia JS-32265. 1 disc.

Having had a success with Company, Stephen Sondheim turned his attention to adapting Ingmar Bergman's Smiles of a summer night, a film, to the stage. The score for this is one of Sondheim's weakest, but does contain the obligatory "Send in the clowns" as well as his accute observations on marriage, infidelity, and family life.

MAME.   Columbia KOS-3000. 1 disc.

Angela Lansbury was the undisputed queen of Broadway when she appeared as the madcap Auntie Mame. This Jerry Herman score has proven to be a favorite with theater aud-iences everywhere, and has served as a vehicle for several actresses like Ginger Rogers, Janis Paige, Susan Hayward, Celeste Holm, etc.   A feature film was made in 1974 with Lucille Ball in the title role, and she quickly showed audiences who loved Lucy, that although talented, the part of Mame was a classic case of bad casting. Angela Lansbury, brings such vibrancy to the role that her songs literally sing themselves, yet they spotlight her exuberance in such numbers as "That's how young I feel", "Boy with a bugle", "Bossom buddies", "It's today", "Open a new window", etc.

MAN OF LA MANCHA. MCA 2018. 1 disc.

   "The impossible dream" has become such
a standard, that it is not known to many
that it originated in this musical, based
on the adventures of Don Quixote and his
trusty servant, Sancho Panza. Audiences
either enjoyed or disliked it--and I must
confess, I was unimpressed with it when I
first saw it on Broadway, and later when
I listened to the original cast recording.
But some things do grow on you, and every
time I hear this, I discover something
to like and appreciate.

THE MUSIC MAN. Capitol SW-990. 1 disc.

   When a charlatan vendor of musical
instruments visits River City, he points
out to the townspeople that the changes
their town is undergoing, can be curbed
by introducing music into the lives of
the wayward youth. Robert Preston was
the showman extraordinaire. His rapid
fire delivery of some of the most complex
lines ever written, are spoken as easily
as some recall their address. Lots of
familiar songs--"Till there was you",
"Seventy six trombones", etc.

MY FAIR LADY. Columbia PS-2015. 1 disc.

   Julie Andrews and Rex Harrison head
up the original Broadway cast recording.
The music is charming, filled with music
that has become familiar over the last
two decades. This was one of the longest
running musicals of all time, and also,
one of the most successful.

OKLAHOMA. Columbia OS-2610. 1 disc.

One of the most important musicals that
Richard Rodgers and Oscar Hammerstein II
ever turned out, it was to revolutionize
the musical theater and subsequent productions would employ Oklahoma as the pro-
totype. It came along at a particularly
right period in our history...our entrance
to World War II. It emphasized simple values,
family, community, and property, the three
of which were inseparable. This is what
our American soldiers were going away to
defend, and many would not return. Still,
even after the war, it remained popular
with audiences around the world. The music,
even today, commands our attention and
interest. From the proud, somewhat boastful
title tune, and the "Oh, what a beautiful
morning" opener, this is a picture of a
rural placid America.   Essential.

OLIVER. RCA LSOD-2004. 1 disc.

The Broadway cast came mostly via way
of the London stage. In London, this Lionel
Bart adaptation of Dicken's Oliver Twist,
had been one of the biggest and most
successful production up to that time. After
more than twenty five hundred performances,
it was brought to Broadway, but it had a
less durable lifetime, only lasting a few
seasons.

PROMISES, PROMISES.   United Artists 9902.
    1 disc.

In the sixties, one of the hottest musical
teams was that of Burt Bacharach and Hal
David. Together, they wrote some of the
biggest songs of that era. When they furnished the songs for this Neil Simon book,
it was assumed that they would find a new
career. But, such was not the case, and
both returned to the top 40 market.

THE SOUND OF MUSIC   Columbia S-32601.
    1 disc.

    Mary Martin has had a lengthy Broadway
stage career, appearing in many of its
most popular attractions--Peter Pan,
South Pacific, and this, probably one
of her best. As Maria Von Trapp she
brought a different dimension to the
role, that was missing in the film.
All the songs are here, but there is
a substantial and variance in interpret-
ation.

SWEENEY TODD.   2-RCA CBL2-3379.   2 discs.

    There has been some change in the musical
theatre of late. Whereas once they were
lightweight fantasies meant to pass away
an evening and then return to the real
world, some of what is being presented up
on stage is far from superficial. Sweeney
Todd, a barber by profession, is based on
a real character. With revenge in his heart,
he teams up with Angela Lansbury, and together
they roast and bake up an assortment of London's
inhabitants. This is a dark musical, but it
bears the unmistakable genius of Stephen
Sondheim.

SWEET CHARITY. Columbia KOS-2900. 1 disc.

    Neil Simon took the script of a famous
Federico Fellini film, Americanized it,
and gave a new lease on life to the delight-
ful Charity Hope Valentine, in the person of
Gwen Verdon. With John McMartin as her
romantic interest, and a supporting cast
that is just short of marvelous, the bouncy
Cy Coleman/Dorothy Fields musical includes
some of the best music ever written for the
Broadway stage.

WEST SIDE STORY.   Columbia JS-32603.   1 disc.

Few musicals have taken the nation by
storm as did this.   With music by Leonard
Bernstein and lyrics by a young newcomer,
Stephen Sondheim, it was hailed as a huge
success when it first appeared in the late
'50's.   Transposing Shakespeare's Romeo
and Juliet into a New York City environment,
instead of feuding families, we are given two
street gangs, the Jets and the Sharks who
are at odds with one another.   Maria and
Tony, lovers from opposite gangs, meet,
fall in love, and endure a tragic fate.
The jazz inspired music is till contemporary.

THE WIZ.   Atlantic 18137.   1 disc.

Black musicals have frequently been popular, and this was no exception.   Based
on The Wizard of Oz, many of the familiar
characters have been retained, but made a
bit more ethnic.   Lots of urban humor and
allusions to city life make this something
adults as well as children can enjoy.   "Ease
on down the road" is but one of the production numbers that keep things interesting.

ALIEN. 20th Century T-593. 1 disc.

Few films shocked so many as did Alien,
one of the most horrifying science fiction
movies ever made. The music was an essential
ingredient of the film, and Jerry Goldsmith's
score was vital. Capturing the gamut of
emotions from tranquility in space to sheer
terror, is no easy thing. But Goldsmith has
succeeded here, and the soundtrack is enjoyable on its own.

AROUND THE WORLD IN 80 DAYS. MCA 2062.
    1 disc.

Victor Young, the composer responsible
for the title tune for this 1956 motion
picture, probably never imagined that he
was writing something that would be a
standard a generation later. The rest of
the score is equally lighthearted and
melodic, with occasional ethnic touches.

BEN-HUR. MGM 1SE-1. 1 disc.

While the music from Ben-Hur is not very well known, this is one of Miklos Rozsa's finest scores. Writing music for a monumental film as complex as this epic, is no easy job. Rozsa, however, is one of the better craftsmen in Hollywood, and he has created a score that is characteristic of his best work (Spellbound, Double Indemnity, Madame Bovary). Richly symphonic, the score also features marches, several sub themes, and the frequently performed "Love theme".

BUTCH CASSIDY AND THE SUNDANCE KID. A&M 4227. 1 disc.

Burt Bacharach who was more well-known for his top 40 song hits and his musical comedy, Promises, Promises, wrote the music for this light hit western. Set in turn of the century America, the film follows the rise and eventual downfall of two amiable rascals who have an affinity for robbing banks. Bacharach's score captures the happy go lucky attitude of the protagonists, as well as providing the hit song, "Raindrops keep fallin' on my head". The waltz in this score is especially lovely.

CABARET. MCA AB-752. 1 disc.

Liza Minnelli can do no wrong, and on this soundtrack recording she is peerless! As far as the great score from the Broadway hit goes, several of the weaker numbers have been left out, and a few new songs have been added ("Maybe this time"). The Kander/Ebb score never sounded so good!

AMELOT. Warner Bros. K-3102. 1 disc.

One of the criticisms levelled against
ollywood is that when Broadway musicals
re brought to the screen, it is hard to
iscern the original score due to orch-
stral overkill. This is one such case,
ith so many instruments used, that the
rchestra must have been huge. The score
as been amplified, segments of certain
hemes are reprised as on-screen filler,
ut the singing of Richard Harris and Vanessa
edgrave is quite acceptable, and all
ontribute to an enjoyment of the score.

AROUSEL. Capitol SW-694. 1 disc.

One of Rodgers and Hammerstein's more
nchanting scores, this soundtrack recording
ith Gordon McRae and Shirley Jones exudes
charm generally missing in most record-
ngs of this family favorite. From the
Carousel Waltz" to "You'll never walk
lone", each song is especially poignant.

LOSE ENCOUNTERS OF THE THIRD KIND. Arista
   9500. 1 disc.

John Williams must be one of Hollywood
usiest composers nowadays. In an age when
ost soundtrack recordings utilize top 40
its or songs from other sources, it is
easuring to find that there are still some
ractitioners of the old school of film
coring (in the tradition of say, Max
teiner, Bernard Herrmann, or Alfred Newman).
he main title and theme, plus "The Conversation"
re among the most familiar tracks.

DAYS OF HEAVEN. Pacific Arts-128. 1 disc.

Italy has given us some terrific screen composers such as Nino Rota and Ennio Morricone. This turn of the century love story captures the essence of an innocent American midwest.

THE DEER HUNTER. Capitol S00-11940. 1 disc.

The war in Vietnam was ignored by Hollywood for nearly a decade. It was not until then that filmmakers felt it a suitable subject for a film. The score of Michael Cimino's Oscar winning film is more about friendships and relationships than the war, yet Vietnam plays an integral role.

DR. ZHIVAGO. MGM 1SE-6. 1 disc.

Sweeping panoramas of golden wheatfields, snow covered tundra, and a romance caught in the throes of the Russian revolution--that is how I remember the film, Dr. Zhivago. "Lara's theme", which did not originally have lyrics, became a top 40 hit, "Somewhere my love" for Ray Conniff, Andy Williams, and others. It is the most haunting number in this Maurice Jarre score, and long after one has forgotten the film's storyline, this one single melody can bring it all back. While some native Russian melodies are incorporated into the score, there is a lot of original material as well.

EXODUS. RCA LSO-1058. 1 disc.

The Ernest Gold score celebrating the founding of the state of Israel, includes the popular title theme. This is heard in several sub themes that reappear.

FUNNY GIRL. Columbia JS-3220. 1 disc.

Regardless of what anyone tells you,
the soundtrack version of Funny Girl is
better than the Broadway original cast
recording. The film version was tight-
ened, songs were dropped, numbers added,
and it became a showcase for Barbra
Streisand. Without her singing, it is
doubtful that this film could ever have
become a hit. Simply stated, she is the
show. The Fanny Brice story was told
earlier as Rose of Washington Square
with Alice Faye, although in a thinly
disguised form. The non-singing demands
made upon Omar Sharif result in a charming
portrait of a gambling rake who eventually
married the leading lady of the Ziegfeld
Follies. The closing of the film with
"My Man" provides Ms. Streisand with one
of the screen's great laments.

GIGI. MGM S-3641ST. 1 disc.

Lerner and Loewe who had hit paydirt
on Broadway with My Fair Lady were asked
to write music and lyrics for the story
of a turn of the century coquette who
would not settle for anything less than
marriage. A lovely score, it featured
the talents of Leslie Caron, who had
essayed the role in London, though in a
non-singing capacity. Louis Jourdan,
Maurice Chevalier, and Hermione Gingold
were also billed.

THE GRADUATE.   Columbia JS-3180.   1 disc.

Hollywood had always made movies for audiences, but in the sixties, people started talking about the "youth film". The post war baby boom was of movie going age, and producers lost no time in making films that catered to this generation, such as Easy Rider. Since elaborate symphonic scores were not an essential element of these films, filmmakers looked to the popular media, and discovered a gold mine that had previously gone untapped--radio. Top 40 radio has since, provided us with the music for most of our films. It is lamentable, that so few orig-inal motion picture scores are being written today. The Graduate featured one of the best soundtrack scores of a non-musical film. Featuring the music of Simon and Garfunkel, it brought their music to the attention of a fickle public, and in short course, several films were using soft folk guitar vocals as well. This film featured "Mrs. Robinson", "Scarborough Fair", and "Sounds of Silence".

GREASE.   2-RSO-4002.   2 discs.

Audiences were betting that John Travolta could not repeat his success in Saturday Night Fever with this tepid adaptation of the stage production that has literally become a cult item. However, they were wrong, since Grease turned out to be very popular indeed. Teaming Olivia Newton-John with Travolta provided them with the opportunity to vocalize together. Many of the songs from the original show were thrown out. Some original material was added, and the book was substantially altered. The production credits were spread out among several recognizable names in the pop music industry.

JAWS. MCA-2087. 1 disc.

When this tale of a killer shark first appeared on the nation's theater screens, the music was singled out as one of its most effective elements. With a subtle and simple rhythm, it kept pace with our beating hearts, almost serving as an alarm that danger was on the horizon. The music darts in and out of a complex tapestry of fear. For those with that nagging question in the back of their minds, yes, this is the same John Williams who is the conductor of the Boston Pops, having succeeded the late Arthur Fiedler.

JESUS CHRIST SUPERSTAR. 2-MCA 11000. 2 discs.

This is one of those on-screen disasters that was nevertheless popular with the public due to the familiar score and the songs that had previously been hits--i.e., "I don't know how to love him". Ted Neely portrayed Jesus, repeating a role he had previously played on stage in Los Angeles. Other cast members were very convincing in their roles. But it is the music in this soundtrack that will probably endure long after the movie has been forgotten.

THE KING AND I. Capitol SW-740. 1 disc.

One of the first musicals to exploit Cinemascope and fill the screen with action, The King and I had previously been on the screen in a dramatic version staring Rex Harrison. But it was Yul Brynner at his imperious best that stole the show as the King of Siam. The popular Rodgers and Hammerstein score charmed all, and while it is not Deborah Kerr's voice on the album, this is one of those classic soundtracks that belongs in every collection.

LADY SINGS THE BLUES. 2-Motown 7-758.
2 discs.

Diana Ross does her own singing, and
grateful we can be for that. In capturing
the story of Billie Holliday, she has chosen
to perform many of the songs the late blues
singer included in her repertoire. She
does not attempt to mimic Miss Holliday,
but she very definitely makes the songs
her own.

LOVE STORY. Paramount 6002. 1 disc.

What can you say about a film that
made a lot of money? Well, in this case,
not much needs to be said, except that
the Francis Lai score is among the most
lachrymose examples of music ever set to
film. The main theme has become so well
known, that many people mistakenly believe
that it won "Best Song" in the Oscar
sweepstakes. Actually, the entire score
won. The popular song, "Where do I begin"
did not emerge until much later. Taken
as a whole, the score is deserving of
inclusion in even the most basic collection.

A MAN AND A WOMAN. United Artists 5147.
1 disc.

Francis Lai is definitely of the
romantic school of film scoring. As can
be heard in the soundtrack of this French
film, various elements are incorporated
into his music--however, overall it retains
a romantic flavor. By all means obtain
the French language version of the soundtrack. An English language edition exists,
but this is such a pallid recording in
comparison to the original, that even
non-purists would detect a noticeable
difference.

MIDNIGHT COWBOY.   United Artists 5198.
1 disc.

        So many modern films deal with
alienation, loneliness, and fear in the
urban environment. This study of a
would-be male prostitute with a heart
of gold, featured one of the best scores
ever written by John Barry. The title
theme recalled images of a lonely cowboy
walking up a dusty street, only in this
case it was a pretend cowboy in the very
mean streets of Manhattan. "Everybody's
talkin'" by Harry Nillson was a big hit
due to its appearance in the film.

MY FAIR LADY.   Columbia JS-2600. 1 disc.

        When Hollywood brought My Fair Lady
to the screen, they overlooked Julie
Andrews in favor of the more recognizable
star, Audrey Hepburn. Rex Harrison was
retained from the original Broadway cast,
as were Wilfrid Hyde-White and Stanley
Holloway. The music was even flashier
than on stage. What Hollywood does with
a symphony orchestra from time to time
can be unreal. Only the best studio
musicians were employed for the film,
resulting in one of the best scored
soundtracks ever recorded.

OKLAHOMA.   Capitol SWAO-595. 1 disc.

        Time has not dimmed the luster on
this musical. Pure Americana, the Rodgers
and Hammerstein score set a nation singing
and boasting about its past. By the time
this successful Broadway musical was filmed,
Gordon MacRae and Shirley Jones were the
on-screen sweethearts, warbling the songs
in such a fresh manner that it was hard
to believe that it had been almost fifteen
years since Oklahoma had first appeared.

OLIVER! RCA COSD-5501. 1 disc.

Be thankful that Hollywood is some-
times excessive! In this case, the charming
musical version of Charles Dickens' Oliver
Twist had been a big hit in London, but
the Lionel Bart tuner had only enjoyed
moderate success on Broadway. Scored in
a grandiose and lavish manner by John
Green, it called up many of the loving
musical gimmicks of the greatest musicals.
The score was often dwarfed by the magnitude
of the production numbers--a case in point
being the "Consider yourself" number, which
continued chorus after chorus, ad infinitum.
Still, individual numbers are extremely
enjoyable due to an effervescent Shani
Wallis, a crafty Ron Moody, and all the
power an orchestra can muster.

PATTON. 20th Century-Fox 902. 1 disc.

Jerry Goldsmith's rousing march
celebrates the heroic deeds and adventures
of General George S. Patton. The other
parts of the soundtrack, while not as
familiar, do capture the complexities
of war and the after effects of battle.
As a dividend, the entire speech Patton
(George C. Scott) delivers to his troops
at the beginning of the film, has been
included.

THE PINK PANTHER. RCA ANL1-1389. 1 disc.

Henry Mancini was one of Hollywood's
most prolific scorers of film music through-
out most of the sixties. Still working,
he has in the past decade reduced the
number of his compositions. This score
features madcap melodies, romantic numbers,
elusive fragments, and vocals as well.

ROCKY. United Artists LA-693-G. 1 disc.

As one would expect, the music for a
film about a prize fighter is anything
but maudlin. Bill Conti, has composed
a score that has become almost a cliche
through overuse. The "Rocky theme" ("Gonna
fly now"), must be the second most heard
piece of movie music, after Star Wars.
There are lots of jazz music influences
in the score, and it is difficult to recall
other scores that used jazz in the same
manner. Of course, jazz was frequently
employed in the soundtracks of films in
the 50's and 60's, but in recent years
it has all but been replaced by second
hand hits.

ROMEO AND JULIET. Capitol ST-400. 1 disc.

The score for Franco Zefferelli's
telling of Shakespeare's tragic tale of
the star-crossed lovers of Verona, was
given considerable attention. Lucky for
us that Nino Rota was chosen, since among
film composers, he is without a doubt,
one of the best. While most of the compositions are his own, he has selected to
use music of the time, interweaving the
two into a cohesive entity. The title
theme was later lyricized as "A Time For
Us", which became a hit for Andy Williams,
Johnny Mathis, and others. Brief excerpts
of dialogue are also included, as a sort
of aural bookmark telling you where in
the story you are.

SATURDAY NIGHT FEVER. 2-RSO 4001. 2 discs.

     The disco beat of the music by the Bee Gees and other assorted individuals and groups form the nucleus around which other elements of the film depended. The storyline involves a young man, who feels alienated from his family, friends, and society. Trapped in a dead end job in a paint store, he has reached the finish line in his race with life. But, while he may not be much by day, at night all is reversed, and he becomes a desirable sex object and the undisputed king of the local disco. Without the powerful disco score by the Bee Gees, John Travolta might not have become the big star he is today.

SINGIN' IN THE RAIN/EASTER PARADE. 2-MGM SES-40. 2 discs.

     Many knowledgeable film critics argue that Singin' in the rain may well be the best movie musical ever. Certainly, listening to the score, it would be difficult to disagree. Donald O'Connor, Debbie Reynolds, and Gene Kelly each have specialty numbers, as well as their ensemble rendition of the title song. Easter Parade is a Judy Garland-Fred Astaire musical fantasy, which is as sweet as a wedding cake. Directed by Vincente Minnelli, it too is considered a classic, but not on the same level as the former.

THE SOUND OF MUSIC. RCA LSOD-2005. 1 disc.

This Rodgers and Hammerstein musical was a big hit for Julie Andrews, repeating with a sincere sweetness, all the songs of the original stage production (with Mary Martin), that audiences had come to know and love--"Do Re Me", "Edelweiss", "Something Good", "My Favorite Things", and "Climb Ev'ry Mountain". Irwin Kostal scored for the screen, and did a very good job adapting music he did not initially compose.

SOUTH PACIFIC. RCA LSO-1032. 1 disc.

At times, it appears as though Rodgers and Hammerstein were the only composers in America! This wartime story set in the South Pacific featured Mitzi Gaynor and Rosanno Brazzi (with the voice of Ezio Pinza on the musical numbers). The soundtrack recording was opened up a bit more orchestrally than the stage version. If one were to pick between the stage and film cast recordings, opting for the former would be the wisest move.

STAR WARS. 20th Century-Fox 2-541. 2 discs.

John Williams, is probably best known for this score, which probably makes him Hollywood's best known composer of film music. Not only has he scored Jaws, Close Encounters of the Third Kind, and Superman, but his "Star Wars" theme is fast approaching the ubiquitous level of "Also Sprach Zarathustra", first heard in 2001: A Space Odyssey. On practically any weekend, the "Star Wars" theme can be heard during half time at football games, community parades, high school concerts, the supermarket, etc. Most screen musicians are quite content to have composed one great score in their career. But one gets the idea that Williams still hasn't written his most memorable composition yet.

37

THE STING.   MCA 2040.   1 disc.

   Using the music of American composer
Scott Joplin, Marvin Hamlisch almost
singlehandedly revived the public interest
in the work of this forgotten Black artist.
Joplin is best known for the hundreds of
piano rags he composed around the turn
of the century.

SUPERMAN.   Warner Bros. 2BSK-3257.   2 discs.

   With both Close Encounters of the Third
Kind and Star Wars under his musical belt,
John Williams was the natural choice to
compose the music for the film version of
Superman.   Like the title character, the
music is heroic in tone, recalling in small
measure, the "Star Wars Theme".   There is
also a lot of incidental scoring which
illustrates Williams' way with music.

TAXI DRIVER.   Arista 4079.   1 disc.

   This was one of the final film scores
composed by Bernard Herrmann, and as such,
is a fiting capstone to an illustrious
career filled with memorable scores.   Featuring wailing brass, and snatches of atonal
paraphrases from the main recurring theme,
the violence of life in the inner city is
ever present.   Loneliness and alienation
are evident in the music, reflecting thse
aspects of the film's storyline.

THE TEN COMMANDMENTS. United Artists
LA304-G. 1 disc.

When Cecil B. DeMille put his name
on a film, to movie audiences it was a
sure sign that this would be an epic of
masterful proportions. The Ten Commandments, is such a film, based on the Bible
and other sources, it tells of Moses and
his search for the promised land, the
flight of the Israelites from Egypt, etc.
The music, scored by Elmer Bernstein,
captures the sweep and epic nature of the
film, especially the victorious flight
of the Israelites from their captivity.

THAT'S ENTERTAINMENT. 2-MCA-11002. 2 discs.

The Metro-Goldwyn-Mayer studios pro-
duced some of the most memorable film musicals ever made, and this soundtrack
recording serves as an appropriate memory
jolter of highlights from several--Gigi,
Singin' in the Rain, Showboat, Meet Me
in St. Louis, An American in Paris, etc.
Because the studio boasted of having more
stars than there are in heaven, they
attempted to use even their dramatic names
from time to time--often with disastrous
results. To anyone who loves the film
musical, this nostalgia-laden title is
a must. Fortunately for us they have not
attempted to squeeze everything onto a
single disc, but have rather generously
included entire production numbers instead
of excerpts. The result is this marvelous
two record set that all collections will
want to include in their holdings.

2001: A SPACE ODYSSEY. MGM S1E-13. 1 disc.

    Stanley Kubrick directed this space
epic, set in the not too distant future.
The music he chose, while not original,
was nevertheless quite striking, and even
now one can recall the satellite-space
station drifting in the black ocean of
space while the "Blue Danube Waltz" played
in the background.

THE UMBRELLAS OF CHERBOURG. Phillips 616.
1 disc.

    A delightful operetta for the screen,
with music by Michel Legrand. The French
language musical tells of a bittersweet
love affair between a young garage mechanic
and the daughter of a shopkeeper in the
port city of Cherbourg. The entire story
is told in song, and often one is amazed
how well the action flows. It is a very
romantic score, and those who favor realism,
will probably find this charming gem un-
appealing.

THE WAY WE WERE. Columbia JS-32830. 1 disc.

    The music is by Marvin Hamlisch, and
the lyrics by the team of Marilyn and Alan
Bergman. Between themselves, they have
won enough Oscars to fill a large mantle.
This nostalgic love story set over a period
of several decades, explores a variety of
themes. The music is often reflective of
the period--"Red Sails in the Sunset", "In
the Mood", etc. Barbra Streisand sings the
title tune, which won the Academy Award in
that year's Oscarfest.

WEST SIDE STORY. Columbia JS-2070. 1 disc.

While the voices on the soundtrack are not those of the stars of the film (Natalie Wood and Richard Beymer), the Stephen Sondheim/ Leonard Bernstein score never sounded so powerful. There is more fire to the numbers, and of course, Rita Moreno is priceless. Still, it almost takes the film soundtrack to convince you of the timeless nature of this inner-city Romeo and Juliet motif, to say nothing about one of Hollywood's truly greatest recordings.

BIBLIOGRAPHY

A musical on record is forever! But there often comes a time when one wishes to know something about the musical as a whole. Reading the libretto can often clarify an allusion to something in the score. For those who wish to read the books of several musicals, I am offering the following list. It is by no means comprehensive or all-inclusive. But it at least serves as a beginning point for additional individual study.

ANYONE CAN WHISTLE. Book by Arthur Laurents, music and lyrics by Stephen Sondheim. Random House, 1965.

APPLAUSE. Book by Betty Comden and Adolph Green, music by Charles Strouse, lyrics by Lee Adams. Random House, 1971.

BYE BYE BIRDIE. Book by Michael Stewart, lyrics of Lee Adams, music by Charles Strouse. DBS Publications, 1962.

CARNIVAL. Book by Michael Stewart, music and lyrics by Bob Merrill. DBS Publications, 1968.

COMPANY. Book by George Furth, music and lyrics by Stephen Sondheim. Random House, 1970.

DO I HEAR A WALTZ? Book by Arthur Laurents,
    music by Richard Rodgers, lyrics by Ste-
    phen Sondheim. Random House, 1966.

FANNY. Book by S. N. Behrman and Joshua
    Logan, music and lyrics by Harold Rome.
    Random House, 1954.

THE FANTASTICKS. Book and lyrics by Tom
    Jones, music by Harvey Schmidt. Drama
    Book Shop, 1964.

FOLLIES. Book by James Goldman, music and
    lyrics by Stephen Sondheim. Random
    House, 1971.

FUNNY GIRL. Book by Isobel Lennart, music
    by Jule Styne, lyrics by Bob Merrill.
    Random House, 1964.

GOLDEN BOY. Book by Clifford Odets and
    William Gibson, lyrics by Lee Adams,
    music by Charles Strouse. Atheneum, 1965.

GYPSY. Book by Arthur Laurents, music by
    Jule Styne, lyrics by Stephen Sondheim.
    Random House, 1960.

HELLO, DOLLY! Book by Michael Stewart,
    music and lyrics by Jerry Herman. DBS,
    1966.

I CAN GET IT FOR YOU WHOLESALE. Book by
    Jerome Weidman, music and lyrics by
    Harold Rome. Random House, 1962.

THE KING AND I. Book and lyrics by Oscar
    Hammerstein II, music by Richard Rodgers.
    Random House, 1951.

LADY IN THE DARK. Book by Moss Hart,
    lyrics by Ira Gershwin, music by Kurt
    Weill. Random House, 1941.

MAME. Book by Jerome Lawrence and Robert
    E. Lee, music and lyrics by Jerry Herman.
    Random House, 1967.

MAN OF LA MANCHA. Book by Dale Wasserman,
    lyrics by Joe Darion, music by Mitch
    Leigh. Random House, 1966.

THE MUSIC MAN. Book by Meredith Willson,
    music and lyrics by Meredith Willson.
    Putnam, 1958.

MY FAIR LADY. Adaptation and lyrics by Alan
    Jay Lerner, music by Frederick Loewe.
    Coward-McCann, 1956.

NEW GIRL IN TOWN. Book by George Abbott,
    music and lyrics by Bob Merrill. Random
    House, 1958.

NO STRINGS. Book by Samuel Taylor, music
    and lyrics by Richard Rodgers. Random
    House, 1962.

OKLAHOMA! Book by Oscar Hammerstein II,
    music and lyrics by Richard Rodgers.
    Random House, 1943.

ON A CLEAR DAY YOU CAN SEE FOREVER. Book
    by Alan Jay Lerner, music by Burton Lane.
    Random House, 1966.

PACIFIC OVERTURES. Book by John Weidman,
    music and lyrics by Stephen Sondheim.
    Dodd, Mead & Co., 1976.

THE PAJAMA GAME. Book by George Abbott
    and Richard Bissell, music and lyrics
    by Richard Adler and Jerry Ross. Random
    House, 1954.

PIPE DREAM. Book and lyrics by Oscar
    Hammerstein II, music by Richard Rodgers.
    Viking Press, 1956.

PIPPIN. Book by Roger O. Hirson. Drama
    Book Specialists, 1975.

PROMISES, PROMISES. Book by Neil Simon,
    music by Burt Bacharach, lyrics by Hal
    David. Random House, 1969.

1776. Book by Peter Stone, music and lyrics
    by Sherman Edwards. The Viking Press,
    1970.

THE SOUND OF MUSIC. Book by Howard Lindsay, lyrics by Oscar Hammerstein II, music by Richard Rodgers. Random House, 1960.

SWEET CHARITY. Book by Neil Simon, music by Cy Coleman, lyrics by Dorothy Fields. Random House, 1966.

TENDERLOIN. Book by Jerome Weidman and George Abbott, music by Jerry Bock, lyrics by Sheldon Harnick. Random House, 1961.

THE UNSINKABLE MOLLY BROWN. Book by Richard Morris, lyrics and music by Meredith Willson. G. P. Putnam's Sons, 1961.

WEST SIDE STORY. Book by Arthur Laurents, music by Leonard Bernstein, lyrics by Stephen Sondheim. Random House, 1958.

ZORBA! Book by Joseph Stein, lyrics by Fred Ebb, music by John Kander. Random House, 1969.

TEN GREAT MUSICALS OF THE AMERICAN THEATRE. Edited by Stanley Richards. Chilton Book Co.

Includes: OF THEE I SING; PORGY AND BESS; ONE TOUCH OF VENUS; BRIGADOON; KISS ME, KATE; WEST SIDE STORY; GYPSY; FIDDLER ON THE ROOF; 1776; COMPANY.

GREAT MUSICALS OF THE AMERICAN THEATRE,
  VOLUME 2. Edited by Stanley Richards.
  Chilton Book Co., 1976.

  Includes: A LITTLE NIGHT MUSIC; APPLAUSE;
  CABARET; CAMELOT; FIORELLO!; LADY IN THE
  DARK; LEAVE IT TO ME; LOST IN THE STARS;
  MAN OF LA MANCHA; WONDERFUL TOWN.

APPENDIX

ACADEMY AWARD WINNERS

Presented annually in the spring by the Academy of Motion Picture Arts and Sciences, the Oscars honor the best work of the previous year. What follows is a listing only of the musical awards.

1934
    Best Song: "The Continental"
    Best Scoring: ONE NIGHT OF LOVE

1935
    Best Song: "Lullaby of Broadway"
    Best Scoring: THE INFORMER

1936
    Best Song: "The Way You Look Tonight"
    Best Scoring: ANTHONY ADVERSE

1937
    Best Song: "Sweet Leilani"
    Best Scoring: ONE HUNDRED MEN AND A GIRL

1938
    Best Song: "Thanks For the Memory"
    Best Scoring: ALEXANDER'S RAGTIME BAND
                   (Alfred Newman)
    Best Original Score: THE ADVENTURES OF
            ROBIN HOOD (Erich Wolfgang Korngold)

1939
    Best Song: "Over the Rainbow"
    Best Score: STAGECOACH (Richard Hageman,
       Frank Harling, John Leipold, Leo Shuken)
    Best Original Score: THE WIZARD OF OZ
       (Herbert Stothart)

1940
    Best Song: "When You Wish Upon a Star"
    Best Score: TIN PAN ALLEY (Alfred Newman)
    Best Original Score: PINOCCHIO (Leigh
       Harline, Paul J. Smith, Ned Washington)

1941
    Best Song: "The Last Time I Saw Paris"
    Best Dramatic Score: ALL THAT MONEY CAN
       BUY (Bernard Herrmann)
    Best Musical Score: DUMBO (Frank Churchill
       Oliver Wallace)

1942
    Best Song: "White Christmas"
    Best Dramatic or Comedy Score: NOW, VOYAGE
       (Max Steiner)
    Best Musical Score: YANKEE DOODLE DANDY
       (Ray Heindorf, Heinz Roemheld)

1943
    Best Song: "You'll Never Know"
    Best Dramatic or Comedy Score: THE SONG OF
       BERNADETTE (Alfred Newman)
    Best Musical Score: THIS IS THE ARMY (Ray
       Heindorf)

1944
    Best Song: "Swinging on a Star"
    Best Dramatic or Comedy Score: SINCE YOU
       WENT AWAY (Max Steiner)
    Best Musical Score: COVER GIRL (Carmen
       Dragon, Morris Stoloff)

1945
  Best Song: "It Might As Well Be Spring"
  Best Dramatic or Comedy Score: <u>SPELLBOUND</u>
      (Miklos Rozsa)
  Best Musical Score: <u>ANCHORS AWEIGH</u>
      (Georgie Stoll)

1946
  Best Song: "On the Atchison, Topeka and
              Santa Fe"
  Best Dramatic or Comedy Score: <u>THE BEST
  YEARS OF OUR LIVES</u> (Hugo Friedhofer)
  Best Musical Score: <u>THE JOLSON STORY</u>
      (Morris Stoloff)

1947
  Best Song: "Zip-a-dee-doo-dah"
  Best Dramatic or Comedy Score: <u>A DOUBLE
  LIFE</u> (Miklos Rozsa)
  Best Musical Score: <u>MOTHER WORE TIGHTS</u>
      (Alfred Newman)

1948
  Best Song: "Buttons and Bows"
  Best Dramatic or Comedy Score: <u>THE RED
  SHOES</u> (Brian Easdale)
  Best Musical Score: <u>EASTER PARADE</u> (Johnny
  Green and Roger Edens)

1949
  Best Song: "Baby, It's Cold Outside"
  Best Dramatic or Comedy Score: <u>THE HEIRESS</u>
      (Aaron Copland)
  Best Musical Score: <u>ON THE TOWN</u> (Roger
  Edens, Lennie Hayton)

1950
  Best Song: "Mona Lisa"
  Best Dramatic or Comedy Score: <u>SUNSET
  BOULEVARD</u> (Franz Waxman)
  Best Musical Score: <u>ANNIE GET YOUR GUN</u>
      (Adolph Deutsch, Roger Edens)

1951

Best Song: "In the Cool, Cool, Cool
     of the Evening"
Best Dramatic or Comedy Score: A PLACE
     IN THE SUN (Franz Waxman)
Best Musical Score: AN AMERICAN IN PARIS
     (Johnny Green, Saul Chaplin)

1952

Best Song: "High Noon (Do Not Forsake
     Me, Oh My Darlin')"
Best Dramatic or Comedy Score: HIGH
     NOON (Dimitri Tiomkin)
Best Musical Score: WITH A SONG IN MY
     HEART (Alfred Newman)

1953

Best Song: "Secret Love"
Best Dramatic or Comedy Score: LILI
     (Bronislau Kaper)
Best Musical Score: CALL ME MADAM
     (Alfred Newman)

1954

Best Song: "Three Coins in the Fountain"
Best Dramatic or Comedy Score: THE HIGH
     AND THE MIGHTY (Dimitri Tiomkin)
Best Musical Score: SEVEN BRIDES FOR
     SEVEN BROTHERS (Adolph Deutsch, Saul
     Chaplin)

1955

Best Song: "Love is a Many-Splendored Thing'
Best Dramatic or Comedy Score: LOVE IS A
     MANY-SPLENDORED THING (Alfred Newman)
Best Musical Score: OKLAHOMA! (Robert
     Russell Bennett, Jay Blackton, Adolph
     Deutsch)

1956
    Best Song: "Whatever Will Be, Will Be (Que
        Sera, Sera)"
    Best Dramatic or Comedy Score: AROUND THE
        WORLD IN 80 DAYS (Victor Young)
    Best Musical Score: THE KING AND I (Alfred
        Newman, Ken Darby)

1957
    Best Song: "All the Way"
    Best Musical Score: THE BRIDGE ON THE RIVER
        KWAI (Malcolm Arnold)

1958
    Best Song: "Gigi"
    Best Dramatic or Comedy Score: THE OLD MAN
        AND THE SEA (Dimitri Tiomkin)
    Best Musical Score: GIGI (Andre Previn)

1959
    Best Song;   "High Hopes"
    Best Dramatic or Comedy Score; BEN-HUR
        (Miklos Rozsa)
    Best Musical Score; PORGY AND BESS (Andre
        Previn, Ken Darby)

1960
    Best Song: "Never on Sunday"
    Best Dramatic or Comedy Score: EXODUS
        (Ernest Gold)
    Best Musical Score: SONG WITHOUT END (Morris
        Stoloff, Harry Sukman)

1961
    Best Song: "Moon River"
    Best Dramatic or Comedy Score; BREAKFAST
        AT TIFFANY'S (Henry Mancini)
    Best Musical Score: WEST SIDE STORY (Saul
        Chaplin, Johnny Green, Sid Ramin, Irwin
        Kostal)

1962
:   Best Song: "Days of Wine and Roses"
    Best Music Score--Original: <u>LAWRENCE OF ARABIA</u> (Maurice Jarre)
    Best Scoring of Music--Adaptation or Treatment: <u>THE MUSIC MAN</u> (Ray Heindorf)

1963
:   Best Song: "Call Me Irresponsible"
    Best Music Score--Original: <u>TOM JONES</u> (John Addison)
    Best Scoring of Music--Adaptation or Treatment: <u>IRMA LA DOUCE</u> (Andre Previn)

1964
:   Best Song: "Chim Chim Cher-ee"
    Best Music Score--Original: <u>MARY POPPINS</u> (Richard M. Sherman, Robert B. Sherman)
    Best Scoring of Music--Adaptation or Treatment: <u>MY FAIR LADY</u> (Andre Previn)

1965
:   Best Song: "The Shadow of Your Smile"
    Best Music Score--Original: <u>DOCTOR ZHIVAGO</u> (Maurice Jarre)
    Best Scoring of Music--Adaptation or Treatment: <u>THE SOUND OF MUSIC</u> (Irwin Kostal)

1966
:   Best Song: "Born Free"
    Best Music Score--Original: <u>BORN FREE</u> (John Barry)
    Best Scoring of Music--Adaptation or Treatment: <u>A FUNNY THING HAPPENED ON THE WAY TO THE FORUM</u> (Ken Thorne)

1967
Best Song: "Talk To the Animals"
Best Original Music Score: THOROUGHLY
    MODERN MILLIE (Elmer Bernstein)
Best Scoring of Music--Adaptation or
    Treatment: CAMELOT (Alfred Newman,
    Ken Darby)

1968
Best Song: "The Windmills of Your Mind"
Best Original Score (Non-Musical): THE
    LION IN WINTER (John Barry)
Best Musical Picture Score: OLIVER!
    (adapted by John Green)

1969
Best Song: "Raindrops Keep Fallin' On
    My Head"
Best Original Score (Non-Musical): BUTCH
    CASSIDY AND THE SUNDANCE KID (Burt
    Bacharach)
Best Musical Picture Score: HELLO, DOLLY!
    (adapted by Lennie Hayton, Lionel Newman)

1970
Best Song: "For All We Know"
Best Original Score: LOVE STORY (Francis
    Lai)
Best Original Song Score: LET IT BE (music
    and lyrics by The Beatles)

1971
Best Song: "Theme From Shaft"
Best Original Dramatic Score: SUMMER OF
    '42 (Michel Legrand)
Best Scoring, Adaptation and Original Song
    Score: FIDDLER ON THE ROOF (adapted by
    John Williams)

1972
  Best Song: "The Morning After"
  Best Original Dramatic Score: LIMELIGHT
    (Charles Chaplin, Raymond Rasch, Larry
    Russell)
  Best Scoring, Adaptation and Original
    Song Score: CABARET (adapted by Ralph
    Burns)

1973
  Best Song: "The Way We Were"
  Best Original Dramatic Score: THE WAY WE
    WERE (Marvin Hamlisch)
  Best Scoring, Original Song Score and/or
    Adaptation: THE STING (adapted by
    Marvin Hamlisch)

1974
  Best Song: "We May Never Love Like This
    Again:
  Best Original Dramatic Score: THE GODFATHER,
    PART II (Nino Rota, Carmine Coppola)
  Best Scoring, Original Song Score and/or
    Adaptation: THE GREAT GATSBY (adapted
    by Nelson Riddle)

1975
  Best Song: "I'm Easy"
  Best Original Score: JAWS (John Williams)
  Best Scoring, Original Song Score and/or
    Adaptation: BARRY LYNDON (adapted by
    Leonard Rosenman)

1976
  Best Song: "Evergreen"
  Best Original Score: THE OMEN (Jerry
    Goldsmith)
  Best Scoring, Original Song Score and/or
    Adaptation: BOUND FOR GLORY (adapted
    by Leonard Rosenman)

1977
   Best Song: "You Light Up My Life"
   Best Original Score: STAR WARS (John
      Williams)
   Best Scoring, Original Song Score and/or
      Adaptation: A LITTLE NIGHT MUSIC
      (Jonathan Tunick)

1978
   Best Song: "Last Dance"
   Best Original Score: MIDNIGHT EXPRESS
      (Giorgio Moroder)
   Best Scoring, Original Song Score and/or
      Adaptation: THE BUDDY HOLLY STORY
      (adapted by Joe Renzetti)

1979
   Best Song: "It Goes Like It Goes"
   Best Original Score: A LITTLE ROMANCE
      (Georges Delerue)
   Best Scoring, Original Song Score and/or
      Adaptation: ALL THAT JAZZ (adapted
      by Ralph Burns)

GRAMMY AWARD WINNERS

Every year, the National Academy of Recording Arts and Sciences bestows honors on those recordings and recording artists whom the membership feels have made distinguished and outstanding contributions to the industry. Awards are voted on in a variety of categories. The following, have received the record industry's highest honor in the field of soundtrack recordings.

1958
   Best original cast, Broadway or TV:
      THE MUSIC MAN, Meredith Willson
   Best soundtrack album: GIGI, Andre
      Previn

1959
   Best soundtrack album: ANATOMY OF
      A MURDER, Duke Ellington
   Best soundtrack album, original cast:
      PORGY AND BESS, Motion picture cast
   Best Broadway show album: GYPSY (Ethel
      Merman); REDHEAD (Gwen Verdon)

1960
   Best soundtrack music score: EXODUS,
      Ernest Gold, composer
   Best soundtrack original cast: CAN CAN,
      Frank Sinatra, original cast
   Best show album (original cast): THE
      SOUND OF MUSIC (Mary Martin), Richard
      Rodgers, Oscar Hammerstein II, composers

961
Best soundtrack score: BREAKFAST AT
TIFFANY'S, Henry Mancini
Best soundtrack of original cast:
WEST SIDE STORY, Johnny Green, Saul
Chaplin, Sid Ramin, Irwin Kostal
Best original cast show album: HOW
TO SUCCEED IN BUSINESS WITHOUT REALLY
TRYING, Frank Loesser, composer

962
Best original cast show album: NO STRINGS,
original Broadway cast, Richard Rodgers,
composer

963
Best original score: TOM JONES, John
Addison, conductor, composer
Best score original cast show album:
SHE LOVES ME, original cast, composers
Jerry Bock and Sheldon Harnick

964
Best original score: MARY POPPINS, Julie
Andrews, Dick Van Dyke; composers,
Richard M. Sherman and Robert B. Sherman
Best score from an original cast show
album: FUNNY GIRL, Barbra Streisand,
original cast; composer, Jule Styne
and Bob Merrill

1965
Best original score: THE SANDPIPER, Robert
Armbruster Orchestra, composer, Johnny
Mandel
Best score from an original show album:
ON A CLEAR DAY YOU CAN SEE FOREVER,
composers Alan Jay Lerner, Burton
Lane

1966
    Best original score: DOCTOR ZHIVAGO,
       composer, Maurice Jarre
    Best score from an original cast show
       album: MAME, composer Jerry Herman

1967
    Best original score: MISSION IMPOSSIBLE,
       composer, Lalo Schifrin
    Best score from an original cast show
       album: CABARET, composer Fred Ebb
       and John Kander

1968
    Best original score: THE GRADUATE,
       songwriter, Paul Simon, additional
       music, Dave Grusin
    Best score from an original cast show
       album: HAIR, composer Gerome Ragni,
       James Rado, and Galt MacDermott

1969
    Best original score: BUTCH CASSIDY AND
       THE SUNDANCE KID, composer Burt
       Bacharach
    Best score from an original cast show
       album: PROMISES, PROMISES, composer
       Burt Bacharach and Hal David

1970
    Best original score: LET IT BE, composers
       John Lennon, Paul McCartney, George
       Harrison, Ringo Starr
    Best score from original cast show album:
       COMPANY, composer Stephen Sondheim

971
Best original score written for a motion
   picture: SHAFT, composer Isaac Hayes
Best score from an original cast show
   album: GODSPELL, composer, Stephen
   Schwartz

972
Best original score written for motion
   pictures or television: THE GODFATHER,
   composer Nino Rota
Best score from an original cast show
   album: DON'T BOTHER ME, I CAN'T COPE,
   composer Micki Grant, producer Jerry
   Ragavoy

973
Best album of original score, motion picture:
   JONATHAN LIVINGSTON SEAGULL, composer
   Neil Diamond
Best score from an original cast show
   album: A LITTLE NIGHT MUSIC, composer
   Stephen Sondheim, producer Goddard
   Lieberson

974
Best album original score written for a
   motion picture of a television special:
   THE WAY WE WERE, composer Marvin Hamlisch,
   Alan and Marilyn Bergman

975
Best album of original score written for
   motion picture or television special:
   JAWS, composer John Williams

1976
  Album of original score written for a
    motion picture or a television special:
    CAR WASH, Norman Whitfield
  Best cast show album: BUBBLING BROWN
    SUGAR, Hugo and Luigi producers

1977
  Best original score written for motion
    pictures or a television special:
    STAR WARS, John Williams composer
  Best cast show album: ANNIE, Charles
    Strouse, Martin Charnin, composers,
    Larry Morton, Charles Strouse pro-
    ducers

1978
  Best original score written for a motion
    picture or a television special: CLOSE
    ENCOUNTERS OF THE THIRD KIND, John
    Williams composer
  Best cast show album: AIN'T MISBEHAVIN',
    Thomas Fats Waller and others, composers,
    Thomas Z. Shepard, producer

1979
  Best original score written for a motion
    picture or a television special:
    SUPERMAN, John Williams composer
  Best cast show album: SWEENEY TODD, Stephen
    Sondheim composer/lyricist, Thomas Z.
    Shepard producer

THE ANTOINETTE PERRY AWARDS

Presented every year by the League of New York Theaters and Producers, the Tony Awards honor the best productions of the year in both dramatic and musical categories. What follows is a listing in chronological order of the top musical awards given by the League.

1947

Best supporting actor, musical: David Wayne, Finian's Rainbow

1948

Best actress, musical: Grace Hartman, Angel in the Wings
Best actor, musical: Paul Hartman, Angel in the Wings

1949

Best book, musical: Bella and Samuel Spewack, Kiss Me Kate
Best composer and lyricist, musical: Cole Porter, Kiss Me Kate
Best actress, musical: Nanette Fabray, Love Life
Best actor, musical: Ray Bolger, Where's Charley?

1950

Best musical: Oscar Hammerstein II
and Joshua Logan, South Pacific
Best composer: Richard Rodgers,
South Pacific
Best actress, musical: Mary Martin,
South Pacific
Best actor, musical: Ezio Pinza,
South Pacific
Best supporting actress, musical:
Juanita Hall, South Pacific
Best supporting actor, musical: Myron
McCormick, South Pacific

1951

Best musical: Jo Swerling and Abe
Burrows, Guys and Dolls
Best composer and lyricist: Frank
Loesser, Guys and Dolls
Best actress, musical: Ethel Merman,
Call Me Madam
Best actor, musical: Robert Alda,
Guys and Dolls
Best supporting actress, musical:
Isabel Bigley, Guys and Dolls
Best supporting actor, musical:
Russell Nype, Call Me Madam

1952

Best musical: Oscar Hammerstein II,
The King and I
Best actress, musical: Gertrude
Lawrence, The King and I
Best actor, musical: Phil Silvers,
Top Banana
Best supporting actress, musical:
Helen Gallagher, Pal Joey
Best supporting actor, musical:
Yul Brynner, The King and I

953
Best musical: Joseph Fields, Jerome
   Chodorov, Wonderful Town
Best composer: Leonard Bernstein,
   Wonderful Town
Best actress, musical: Rosalind Russell,
   Wonderful Town
Best actor, musical: Thomas Mitchell,
   Hazel Flagg
Best supporting actress, musical: Sheila
   Bond, Wish You Were Here
Best supporting actor, musical: Hiram
   Sherman, Two's Company

954
Best musical: Charles Lederer and Luther
   Davis, Kismet
Best composer: Alexander Borodin, Kismet
Best actress, musical: Dolores Gray,
   Carnival in Flanders
Best actor, musical: Alfred Drake,
   Kismet
Best supporting actress, musical: Gwen
   Verdon, Can-Can
Best supporting actor, musical: Harry
   Belafonte, John Murray Anderson's Almanac

955
Best musical: George Abbott and Richard
   Bissell, The Pajama Game
Best composer and lyricist: Richard
   Adler and Jerry Ross, The Pajama Game
Best actress, musical: Mary Martin,
   Peter Pan
Best actor, musical: Walter Slezak, Fanny
Best supporting actress, musical: Carol
   Haney, The Pajama Game
Best supporting actor, musical: Cyril
   Ritchard, Peter Pan

68

1956

Best musical: George Abbott and Douglass
Wallop, Damn Yankees
Best composer and lyricist: Richard
Adler and Jerry Ross, Damn Yankees
Best actress, musical: Gwen Verdon,
Damn Yankees
Best actor, musical: Ray Walston, Damn
Yankees
Best supporting actress, musical: Lotte
Lenya, The Threepenny Opera
Best supporting actor, musical: Russ
Brown, Damn Yankees

1957

Best musical: Alan Jay Lerner, My Fair
Lady
Best composer: Frederick Loewe, My Fair
Lady
Best actress, musical: Judy Holliday,
Bells are Ringing
Best actor, musical: Rex Harrison, My
Fair Lady
Best supporting actress, musical: Edith
Adams, Li'l Abner
Best supporting actor, musical: Sydney
Chaplin, Bells are Ringing

1958

Best musical: Meredith Willson and
Franklin Lacey, The Music Man
Best composer and lyricist: Meredith
Willson, The Music Man
Best actress, musical: Thelma Ritter,
New Girl in Town/Gwen Verdon, New
Girl in Town
Best actor, musical: Robert Preston,
The Music Man
Best supporting actress, musical:
Barbara Cook, The Music Man
Best supporting actor, musical: David
Burns, The Music Man

1959

Best musical: Herbert and Dorothy Fields, Sidney Sheldon, David Shaw, Redhead

Best actress, musical: Gwen Verdon, Redhead

Best actor, musical: Richard Kiley, Redhead

Best supporting actress, musical: Pat Stanley, Goldilocks; Cast, La Plume de Ma Tante

Best supporting actor, musical: Russell Nype, Goldilocks; Cast, La Plume de Ma Tante

1960

Best musical: Jerome Weidman and George Abbott, Fiorello!

Best composers: Jerry Bock, Fiorello!; Richard Rodgers, The Sound of Music

Best actress, musical: Mary Martin, The Sound of Music

Best actor, musical: Jackie Gleason, Take Me Along

Best supporting actress, musical: Patricia Neway, The Sound of Music

Best supporting actor, musical: Tom Bosley, Fiorello!

Best director, musical: George Abbott, Fiorello!

1961

Best musical: Michael Stewart, Bye Bye Birdie

Best actress, musical: Elizabeth Seal, Irma la Douce

Best actor, musical: Richard Burton, Camelot

Best supporting actress, musical: Tammy Grimes, The Unsinkable Molly Brown

Best supporting actor, musical: Dick Van Dyke, Bye Bye Birdie

Best director, musical: Gower Champion, Bye Bye Birdie

1962
>Best musical: Abe Burrows, Jack Weinstock, Willie Gilbert, How To Succeed in Business Without Really Trying
>Best Composer: Richard Rodgers, No Strings
>Best actress, musical: Anna Maria Alberghetti, Carnival; Diahann Carroll, No Strings
>Best actor, musical: Robert Morse, How To Succeed in Business Without Really Trying
>Best supporting actress, musical: Phyllis Newman, Subways Are For Sleeping
>Best supporting actor, musical: Charles Nelson Reilly, How To Succeed in Business Without Really Trying
>Best director, musical: Abe Burrows, How To Succeed in Business Without Really Trying

1963
>Best musical: Burt Shevelove, Larry Gelbart A Funny Thing Happened on the Way to the Forum
>Best composer and lyricist: Lionel Bart, Oliver!
>Best actress, musical: Vivien Leigh, Tovarich
>Best actor, musical: Zero Mostel, A Funny Thing Happened on the Way to the Forum
>Best supporting actress, musical: Anna Quayle, Stop the world--I want to get off
>Best supporting actor, musical: David Burns, A Funny Thing Happened on the Way to the Forum
>Best director, musical: George Abbott, A Funny Thing Happened on the Way to the Forum

4
Best musical: Michael Stewart, <u>Hello, Dolly!</u>
Best composer and lyricist: Jerry Herman, <u>Hello, Dolly!</u>
Best actress, musical: Carol Channing, <u>Hello, Dolly!</u>
Best actor, musical: Bert Lahr, <u>Foxy</u>
Best supporting actress, musical: Tessie O'Shea, <u>The Girl Who Came to Supper</u>
Best supporting actor, musical: Jack Cassidy, <u>She Loves Me</u>
Best director, musical: Gower Champion, <u>Hello, Dolly!</u>

5
Best musical: Joseph Stein, <u>Fiddler on the Roof</u>
Best composer and lyricist: Jerry Bock and Sheldon Harnick, <u>Fiddler on the Roof</u>
Best actress, musical: Liza Minnelli, <u>Flora, the Red Menace</u>
Best actor, musical: Zero Mostel, <u>Fiddler on the Roof</u>
Best supporting actress, musical: Maria Karnilova, <u>Fiddler on the Roof</u>
Best supporting actor, musical: Victor Spinetti, <u>Oh, What a Lovely War</u>
Best director, musical: Jerome Robbins, <u>Fiddler on the Roof</u>

6
Best musical: Dale Wasserman, <u>Man of La Mancha</u>
Best composer and lyricist: Mitch Leigh, Joe Darion, <u>Man of La Mancha</u>
Best actress, musical: Angela Lansbury, <u>Mame</u>
Best actor, musical: Richard Kiley, <u>Man of La Mancha</u>
Best supporting actress, musical: Beatrice Arthur, <u>Mame</u>
Best supporting actor, musical: Frankie Michaels, <u>Mame</u>
Best director, musical: Albert Marre, <u>Man of La Mancha</u>

1967

    Best musical: Joe Masteroff, <u>Cabaret</u>
    Best composer and lyricist: John Kander,
     Fred Ebb, <u>Cabaret</u>
    Best actress, musical: Barbara Harris,
     <u>The Apple Tree</u>
    Best actor, musical: Robert Preston,
     <u>I Do! I Do!</u>
    Best supporting actress, musical: Peg
     Murray, <u>Cabaret</u>
    Best supporting actor, musical: Joel
     Grey, <u>Cabaret</u>

1968

    Best musical: Arthur Laurents, <u>Hallelujah,</u>
     <u>Baby</u>!
    Best composer and lyricist: Jule Styne,
     Betty Comden and Adolph Green, <u>Hall-</u>
     <u>elujah, Baby</u>!
    Best actress, musical: Patricia Rout-
     ledge, <u>Darling of the Day</u>/Leslie
     Uggams, <u>Hallelujah, Baby</u>!
    Best actor, musical: Robert Goulet, <u>The</u>
     <u>Happy Time</u>
    Best supporting actress, musical: Lillian
     Hayman, <u>Hallelujah, Baby</u>!
    Best supporting actor, musical: Hiram
     Sherman, <u>How Now, Dow Jones</u>
    Best director, musical: Gower Champion,
     <u>The Happy Time</u>

1969

    Best musical: Peter Stone, <u>1776</u>
    Best actress, musical: Angela Lansbury,
     <u>Dear World</u>
    Best actor, musical: Jerry Orbach,
     <u>Promises, Promises</u>
    Best supporting actress, musical: Marian
     Mercer, <u>Promises, Promises</u>
    Best supporting actor, musical: Ronald
     Holgate, <u>1776</u>
    Best director, musical: Peter Hunt, <u>1776</u>

1970

Best musical: Betty Comden, Adolph
Green, Applause
Best actress, musical: Lauren Bacall,
Applause
Best actor, musical: Cleavon Little,
Purlie
Best supporting actress, musical: Melba
Moore, Purlie
Best supporting actor, musical: Rene
Auberjonois, Coco
Best director, musical: Ron Field,
Applause

1971

Best musical: George Furth, Company
Best lyrics, musical: Stephen Sondheim,
Company
Best actress, musical: Helen Gallagher,
No, No, Nanette
Best actor, musical: Hal Linden, The
Rothschilds
Best supporting actress, musical: Patsy
Kelly, No, No, Nanette
Best supporting actor, musical: Keene
Curtis, The Rothschilds
Best director, musical: Harold Prince,
Company

1972

Best musical: John Guare and Mel Shapiro,
Two Gentlemen of Verona
Best book, musical: John Guare, Mel Shapiro,
Two Gentlemen of Verona
Best score, musical: Stephen Sondheim,
Follies
Best actress, musical: Alexis Smith,
Follies

1972 (cont'd.)
   Best actor, musical: Phil Silvers,
      A Funny Thing Happened on the Way
      to the Forum
   Best supporting actress, musical: Linda
      Hopkins, Inner City
   Best supporting actor, musical: Larry
      Blyden, A Funny Thing Happened on the
      Way to the Forum
   Best director, musical: Harold Prince,
      Follies

1973
   Best musical: Hugh Wheeler, A Little
      Night Music
   Best book, musical: Hugh Wheeler, A
      Little Night Music
   Best score, musical: Stephen Sondheim,
      A Little Night Music
   Best actress, musical: Glynis Johns,
      A Little Night Music
   Best actor, musical: Ben Vereen, Pippin
   Best supporting actress, musical:
      Patricia Elliot, A Little Night Music
   Best supporting actor, musical: George
      S. Irving, Irene
   Best director, musical: Bob Fosse,
      Pippin

1974
   Best musical: Robert Nemiroff and Charlotte
      Zaltzberg, Raisin
   Best book, musical: Hugh Wheeler, Candide
   Best score, musical: Frederick Loewe,
      music, Alan Jay Lerner, lyrics, Gigi
   Best actress, musical: Virginia Capers,
      Raisin
   Best actor, musical: Christopher Plummer,
      Cyrano

974 (cont'd.)
   Best supporting actress, musical: Janie
      Sell, Over Here!
   Best supporting actor, musical: Tommy
      Tune, Seesaw
   Best director, musical: Harold Prince,
      Candide

975
   Best musical: William F. Brown, The Wiz
   Best book, musical: James Lee Barrett,
      Peter Udell, and Philip Rose, Shenandoah
   Best score, musical: Charlie Smalls,
      The Wiz
   Best actress, musical: Angela Lansbury,
      Gypsy
   Best actor, musical: John Cullum, Shen-
      andoah
   Best supporting actress, musical: Dee
      Dee Bridgewater, The Wiz
   Best supporting actor, musical: Ted Ross,
      The Wiz
   Best director, musical: Geoffrey Holder,
      The Wiz

976
   Best musical: Thomas Meehan, Annie
   Best book, musical: Thomas Meehan, Annie
   Best score, musical: Charles Strouse,
      music, Martin Charnin, lyrics, Annie
   Best actress, musical: Dorothy Loudon,
      Annie
   Best actor, musical: Barry Bostwick,
      The Robber Bridegroom
   Best supporting actress, musical: Delores
      Hall, Your Arms Too Short To Box With
      God
   Best supporting actor, musical: Lenny
      Baker, I Love My Wife
   Best director, musical: Gene Saks, I
      Love My Wife

1977

Best musical: Emanuel Azenberg, Dasha
Epstein, Jane Gaynor, Ron Dante, Ain't
Misbehavin'

Best book, musical: Betty Comden and
Adolph Green, On the Twentieth Century

Best actress, musical: Liza Minnelli,
The Act

Best actor, musical: John Cullum, On
the Twentieth Century

Best supporting actress, musical: Nell
Carter, Ain't Misbehavin'

Best supporting actor, musical: Kevin
Kline, On the Twentieth Century

Best director, musical: Richard Maltby,
Jr., Ain't Misbehavin'

1978

Best musical: Richard Barr, Charles
Woodward, Robert Fryer, Mary Lea
Johnson, Martin Richards, Sweeney Todd

Best book, musical: Hugh Wheeler, Sweeney
Todd

Best score, musical: Stephen Sondheim,
Sweeney Todd

Best actress, musical: Angela Lansbury,
Sweeney Todd

Best actor, musical: Len Cariou, Sweeney
Todd

Best featured actress, musical: Carlin
Glynn, The Best Little Whorehouse in
Texas

Best featured actor, musical: Henderson
Forsythe, The Best Little Whorehouse
in Texas

Best director, musical: Harold Prince,
Sweeney Todd

1979

Best musical: Evita
Best book, musical: Evita, Tim Rice
Best score, musical: Evita, Andrew
  Lloyd Webber
Best actress, musical: Patti LuPone,
  Evita
Best actor, musical: Jim Dale, Barnum
Best featured actress, musical: Priscilla
  Lopez, A Day in Hollywood/A Night in
  the Ukraine
Best featured actor, musical: Mandy
  Patinkin, Evita
Best director, musical: Harold Prince,
  Evita

INDEX